Introducing Jesus

Peter Scazzero

▶ *Starting an Investigative Bible Study for Seekers*

▶ *With Six Bible Studies*

INTERVARSITY PRESS
DOWNERS GROVE, ILLINOIS 60515

InterVarsity Press is the book-publishing division of InterVarsity Christian Fellowship, a student movement active on campus at hundreds of universities, colleges and schools of nursing in the United States of America, and a member movement of the International Fellowship of Evangelical Students. For information about local and regional activities, write Public Relations Dept., InterVarsity Christian Fellowship, 6400 Schroeder Rd., P.O. Box 7895, Madison, WI 53707-7895.

All Scripture quotations, unless otherwise indicated, are from the Holy Bible, New International Version. Copyright © 1973, 1978, International Bible Society. Used by permission of Zondervan Bible Publishers.

Cover illustration: Roberta Polfus

ISBN 0-8308-1174-5

Printed in the United States of America ∞

Library of Congress Cataloging-in-Publication data

Scazzero, Pete, 1956-
    Introducting Jesus: starting an investigative Bible study for
seekers: with six Bible studies/Pete Scazzero.
      p.   cm.
    Includes bibliographical references.
    ISBN 0-8308-1174-5
    1. Evangelistic work.   2. Non church-affiliated people—Religious
life.   3. Conversion—Biblical teaching.   I. Title.
    BV3793.S33   1991
    269'.2—dc20   91-21911
                                           CIP

15	14	13	12	11	10	9	8	7	6	5	4	3	2	1
03	02	01	00	99	98	97	96	95	94	93	92	91		

To the
Scazzero family
especially
Mom and Dad (Joseph and Francis)
Geri (my wife)
and
Maria (age 5),
Christy (age 4)
and Faith (age 5 months)

1

The Urgent Need

My aunt and uncle had arrived only minutes earlier. Our family was having a small get-together to celebrate our moving into a new apartment in New York City.

"Listen, Peter, I've got to talk to you," whispered my uncle Pete as he dragged his chair toward mine in the dining room.

"Oh, no!" I mumbled to myself.

The bombshell dropped immediately. "I'm so unsatisfied with my life. I hate my job. I'm wasting my life. What should I do?"

I should have been excited about the opportunity to talk with him about Jesus, but I wasn't. I was tired and I would have preferred to keep the conversation light on a night off with my family.

I wanted to be courteous, however, so I asked, "What's up, Uncle Pete?"

His sincere, almost desperate, plea took me by surprise. "I've been in the baking business all my life. I'm going nowhere—making money I have no time to enjoy. I need a change. I'm fed up."

The other conversations at the table stopped. All eyes were fixed on us. He didn't care.

I felt uneasy. Trying to remain casual, I investigated further. "Is there anything happening spiritually in your life?"

"I went to a Bible study for a couple of weeks on Monday nights a few months back. It was on the book of Genesis. It was taught by a seminary professor but I didn't understand it. Anyway, I'm so tired from work that I fall asleep during the class anyway."

My wife and I looked at each other in shock. *He attended a Bible class!* My uncle Pete owns an Italian pastry shop and works every Sunday and holiday. As far as we knew, he never attended church.

I opened up the New Testament to the parable of the sower and the seed (Lk 8:1-15) and asked him a number of observation questions about the seeds that fell on four different types of soil—the path, rock, thorns and good soil.

He ate up the Scriptures like a starving man.

Finally, I applied the passage to him with the question "Which soil best describes the state of your life today?" I was expecting him to say he was like the second or third type of soil that do not bear fruit because of the rocks (which represent testing) and thorns (which are life's worries, riches and pleasures) which choke its growth.

"I'm three going on four!" he blurted out.

Everyone at the table chuckled. He had to be joking. We knew him better than that.

He defended himself with passion. "No kidding. All the money I make illegally, I now give to the church. I don't keep a penny of it."

"Uncle," I muttered under my breath, "I don't think you've quite captured the point of the parable."

We agreed that night to meet in his home once a month for the next three months. That investigative Bible study continued for over a year. My uncle invited neighbors and family, and we averaged between seven to ten people each week.

At the end of that year his twenty-two-year-old son, Peter, Jr., committed his life to Christ. He then led his sister's husband and a number of others to the Lord Jesus.

Meeting the Need
There is an enormous well of unchurched people open to the Lord Jesus waiting to be tapped. Jesus tells us, "The fields . . . are ripe for harvest" (Jn 4:35). Every place we develop relationships—our neighborhoods, work places, colleges or night schools, even annual vacation spots—opens up new opportunities for talking with people about Christ.

While recent scandals have made people extremely sensitive to hypocrisy, religious schemes and a lack of integrity in the church, there remains a sincere longing for God. That yearning, however, is for the authenticity and genuineness found in the God-man Christ Jesus who was a friend of tax collectors and sinners (Lk 15:1-2).

Investigative Bible studies are one excellent means to introduce people to the Lord Jesus through the Scriptures. They are especially powerful for people who are interested in Christianity but who are not yet ready to take the step of becoming a Christian.

This guide is designed to give you practical help in beginning and leading an investigative Bible study. The first part of the guide will give you the skills to start and maintain effective study with non-Christians. In addition, it provides insight into how people make decisions for Christ and what your role can be in that process.

The second part of this guide includes six studies specifically written for use with non-Christians in order to bring them face to face with the living Jesus. I have found most people are willing to do an investigative study with their friends but are looking for material. These studies are written for use with people open and sincerely considering the claims of Christ.

My prayer is that God will use this guide to give you greater
boldness and confidence to introduce your friends and family to the
living Lord Jesus—so that "the light of the knowledge of the glory
of God in the face of Christ" might shine into their hearts (2 Cor
4:6). For as Tertullian (A. D. 160-230) once wrote: "Who can in-
quire into the faith and not embrace it!"

2
Fishing in the
Twentieth Century

Chris and I were best friends. We grew up in the same neighborhood. We enjoyed the same friends. We played the same sports. We even raided the same family refrigerator—mine! Since we were seven years old, Chris had been part of my family. It seemed only right that, after graduating from high school, we should go off to college together.

He was home the night I became a Christian, playing cards and having a few beers with a group of our friends. Until the early hours of the morning I explained to him as best I could how alive Christ was and how he too needed to experience what I had.

He was bored.

I dragged him to Bible studies whenever possible. I explained the gospel to him in a hundred different ways. I begged him to listen to the testimonies of my Christian friends. I prayed for his salvation every day. Meanwhile, he observed firsthand the dramatic transformation the Lord Jesus worked in my life. He watched me for two years.

The problem, however, was that he showed no spiritual hunger or interest. Tall, blonde, blue-eyed and athletic, he seemingly had everything going for him. Tension and frustration entered our relationship. Finally, I grew so frustrated with him that I stopped praying for him and "gave him over" to Satan (even though I had no biblical basis for that).

Following graduation, we continued to play basketball together and remained friends. Since I had given up on any possibility of his becoming a Christian, I no longer spoke to him about Christ.

One summer I was doing a series of investigative Bible studies in my parents' home for my family and friends. I didn't invite Chris, but nonetheless he came when he heard about it.

For four weeks he sat on the couch and said nothing. He refused to answer a question. He refused to participate. He watched our mutual friends evade the implications of the gospel and mock me whenever they had a chance.

"Hey, Pete, where did the animals go to the bathroom on the ark for those forty days?" someone would ask.

Then another would say, "Pete, if God is able to do anything, is he able to make a rock he can't move?"

As far as I could tell, this Bible study was a miserable failure.

The fifth week, however, Chris stood up and announced to the group: "For the past four weeks I have been listening to all of you. I have not been able to get Jesus and the Bible off my mind. Last night I was in turmoil inside. Finally, I said yes to Jesus and gave my life to him. I want you all to know that I'm with Pete now."

Everyone gasped in disbelief, including me. Chris was so unlikely a person to become a Christian that it took him six months to convince even other Christians that he was genuine.

Chris has since led numerous people to Christ and now serves as a leader both in his local church and in a ministry among businesspeople in California.

Chris's story illustrates the enormous potential of investigative Bible studies for the outreach of a church or fellowship. Most non-

Christians are not interested or willing to attend a small group or church event with mostly Christians. They feel uncomfortable and out of place. I couldn't have bribed Chris with money to attend a Christian event. Meeting in my home with other non-Christians, however, wasn't quite as threatening.

What Is an Investigative Bible Study?

An investigative Bible study is a discussion around a passage of Scripture with one primary purpose: to introduce non-Christians to the person of Jesus so that they might submit to him as Savior and Lord of their lives.

An investigative Bible study is primarily concerned with people who know neither the New Testament nor Jesus. The entire meeting is structured and led in such a way that they feel comfortable enough to participate in a Bible discussion.

A church or college small group, on the other hand, is concerned with helping Christians grow in their relationship with Jesus Christ and with one another. They worship, study Scripture, care and pray for one another, and often reach out to nonbelievers. While non-Christians occasionally visit, the format of the meeting rarely changes in order to meet their needs.

In general, the number of Christians present at the investigative Bible study is limited to two. This ensures that it doesn't turn into a "Christian" discussion where non-Christians feel ill at ease. It also prevents Christians from succumbing to the temptation of answering most questions.

The number of non-Christians present, however, can vary from one to twenty. The ideal number for a group seems to be three to eight, but again that depends on the dynamics between the people you've invited. The size of the group also will be determined by your situation and ability to handle the people. Some of my most effective investigative Bible studies have been with only one or two people.

The Power of Scripture

I once made the mistake of inviting a fellow believer (because she was a more mature Christian) to a study with my friends. It had been years since she had had any intimate contact with non-Christians. As a result, she answered all my questions, preached a ten-minute sermon on the wonder of the atonement, and effectively changed the friendly atmosphere in the apartment to one of all-out confrontation. She confused everyone and communicated pride.

"How dare you invite us to a meeting to get preached at!" yelled one of my roommates later that night. "She was so heavy, we didn't understand what she was talking about!"

In investigative studies the Bible serves as the authority, not the leader. The focus is on what the New Testament teaches about Jesus in a given passage. This enables even a new Christian, with the help of a guide, to lead an excellent group. While the leader gives direction through asking questions, everyone is encouraged to participate and interact. The relationship of the Christian(s) to non-Christians is not so much teacher to pupil, but fellow learner to fellow learner.

People soon realize that they too can read the Bible and understand it. This is a radically new experience for many who have never studied the Bible for themselves. For many, God's Word comes alive like never before.

The story about my friend Chris also confirms what Scripture says about itself as being "sharper than any double-edged sword, it penetrates even to dividing soul and spirit, joints and marrow; it judges the thoughts and attitudes of the heart. Nothing in all creation is hidden from God's sight. Everything is uncovered and laid bare before the eyes of him to whom we must give account" (Heb 4:12-13).

People will often deceive themselves and others about their spiritual state. The Scriptures, however, by their very nature, strip people of any pretensions they may have, forcing them to come face to face with the living God.

The Scriptures not only refer to themselves as "living and active" (Heb 4:12), but also as a seed with great power (1 Pet 1:23; Mk 4:14). The Holy Spirit takes this seed and in people just like Chris he mysteriously and supernaturally ignites faith and breathes new life into a spiritually dead person (see Mk 4:26-29). The apostle Peter boldly proclaimed that every believer ultimately has been born again by this seed which never dies, that is, "through the living and enduring word of God" (1 Pet 1:23).

It is this power which you have the opportunity to introduce to others.

3

Friends and Family in Evangelism

When I became a Christian my friends and family would often make comments like:

Did you have to go and become such a fanatic? You've gone overboard with this thing.

The church is full of hypocrites. All they want is your money! Why did you get involved in that?

You must have been really down and out to have gotten into God. Maybe you were just susceptible because of circumstances in your life. It will wear off in time, and you'll be back to normal.

The only people I know who are into that are people who are a mess.

The church you're hanging around sounds like a cult. People are so into God there. How do you know it isn't a cult?

They were skeptical, but they knew something incredible had changed my life. As a result, they would listen to me, watching my every move for inconsistencies or hypocrisy.

I did my best to communicate the gospel effectively to them. I repeatedly shared my testimony, hoping that my excitement would produce fruit. It didn't. If anything, it confused people since they were not having the same experience with God. Almost all concluded it must not be for them.

I listened intently to the altar calls of pastors and evangelists to learn how to present Jesus the right way. They said, "Accept Jesus in your heart." Or "receive him as your Lord and Savior." "Except you be born again, you'll never see the kingdom of God." I treated the words and phrases God used to transform my life like magic. I hoped they would change other's lives as they had mine. But they didn't.

My friends and family also weren't comfortable with either the majority of my new Christian friends or the churches I attended. It represented a totally different culture, with new vocabulary, dress, customs and values. None of them had ever visited an evangelical church. The only Christians they seemed to relate well to were other new Christians like myself!

To further complicate matters, they were not ready to make an immediate decision for Jesus. They needed more information about Jesus and the implications of his claims for their lives. The only solution I could think of was to lead a Bible study in my apartment. A friend and I invited all our friends. I made an agreement with my friends. If they would come to Bible study on Tuesday nights, I would go to the local bar with them on Fridays with the stipulation I could drink 7-Up or Coke.

Twenty showed up at the first meeting. Some drank beer. Others came high on drugs. They joked about sex. They laughed at the fact they were in Bible study for the first time and that I would allow them to share freely their thoughts.

All of them listened.

I selected verses from the Gospels, Revelation, Genesis, Psalms—anything I was familiar with—and explained them the best I could. To them I was a walking Bible, a religious computer program. The reality, however, was that I was a six-month-old Christian, unable to get them into the Scriptures in a way that would cause Jesus to come alive.

In three weeks the Bible study died.

I didn't receive training in investigative Bible studies until a year-and-a-half later. Nevertheless, I knew I was on to something. A close look at the New Testament reveals that one of the reasons the gospel spread so rapidly was because new Christians witnessed powerfully to their friends, relatives, neighbors and coworkers.

Andrew, once he heard John the Baptist's message, immediately found his brother Peter and brought him to Jesus (Jn 1:40-42). The Samaritan woman of John 4 told the people of her town about Jesus (Jn 4:39-42). Jesus instructed the demon-possessed man, once delivered: "Go home to your family and tell them how much the Lord has done for you" (Mk 5:19).

Lydia immediately reached her family network with the gospel (Acts 16:14-15). Luke tells us that the early church met in homes, "praising God and enjoying the favor of all the people. And the Lord added to their number daily those who were being saved" (Acts 2:47).

The Institute of American Church Growth of Pasadena, California, conducted a study on how people have come to Christ and the church. Over 14,000 people in churches were asked the question "What or who was responsible for your coming to Christ and your church?"[1] The remarkable conclusion of this study is seen in the percentage breakdown of the responses. Note what percentage of people came to their new relationship with Christ and their church through each category:

Special Need	1-2%
Walk-In	2-3%
Pastor	5-6%
Visitation	1-2%
Sunday School	4-5%
Evangelistic Crusade	½-1%
Church Program	2-3%
Friend/Relative	75-90%

A Christian is able to so effectively communicate the gospel to their friends and family because they are seeing for themselves the power of the gospel to change a life before their very eyes. Moreover, there is an immediate bond of trust and credibility. The new believer (or Christian friend) is not an outsider from another subculture but one of their own. This is a strategic opportunity.

---

[1]Charles Arn, Donald McGavran, Win Arn, *Growth: A New Vision for the Sunday School* (Pasadena: Church Growth Press, 1980), pp. 75-76.

4

Meeting People Where They Are

To become a Christian, a person must make a decision to receive Jesus Christ as Savior and Lord. That moment, however, of being "born again," of being made spiritually alive in Christ (Eph 2:1-4), is actually preceded by weeks, months and often years of God's work in a person's life.

We cannot regenerate anyone. That is the work of the Holy Spirit (Tit 3:5). Our role is simply to cooperate with God in what he is doing in a person. The apostle Paul understood this when he wrote: "I planted the seed, Apollos watered it, but *God made it grow*. So neither he who plants nor he who waters is anything, but only God, who makes things grow. . . . For we are God's fellow workers" (1 Cor 3:6-9).

There are times when we are talking with people about Christ who are extremely open to becoming Christians (see the Ethiopian eunuch in Acts 8:26-40). They understand a great deal and are ready to make a decision. They only lack information about what it means to repent and believe. Others are not interested in becoming Christians but are open to discuss Jesus (see King Agrippa in

Acts 26:27-32). Still others are antagonistic toward Christ and openly oppose Christianity (see Saul in Acts 8:1-3).

Nearly everyone you and I deal with is somewhere between the stages of being extremely open and extremely closed. Thus, each person requires sensitivity on our part as we seek to cooperate with God. *An investigative Bible study recognizes that while each person who becomes a Christian does make a decision at a specific point in time there is a process which leads a person to that point.*

James Engel has developed a very helpful model for understanding the decision-making process (see diagram A). He makes allowance for the different attitudes and degrees of awareness toward the gospel message. For example, many people are a -6 or -5 on the continuum. To ask them to make a decision for Christ would be foolish. They might, however, be open to attending a Bible study about the person of Jesus. Others are at -3 and -2. Not to summon them to a decision for Christ may be equally foolish. Our role as communicators changes based on where the person is on the experience scale.

Moreover, the model helps us to see that the moment of regeneration (being born again) is only another stage in a person's relationship with God. That person needs to grow into a mature disciple of Jesus Christ (Col 1:28) and responsible member of the church.

For example, for many years I was completely negative toward Jesus and would not engage in even a conversation about him. I was a -9. Nonetheless, God utilized a number of events and people to open me up to the gospel. I left home to live at college. I was challenged by university professors to reflect on the meaning of life. I became disillusioned with the pleasure-seeking lifestyle of my friends. I soon realized there was a void in my life no human relationship could fill. Finally, a good friend whom I respected became a Christian.

Soon, I began asking questions and getting answers. The night

Diagram A: Spiritual-Decision Process

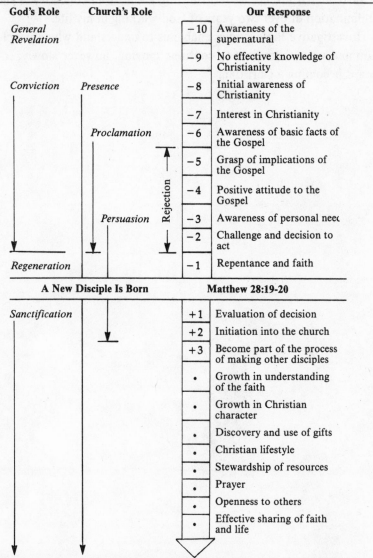

God's Role	Church's Role		Our Response
General Revelation		−10	Awareness of the supernatural
		−9	No effective knowledge of Christianity
Conviction	*Presence*	−8	Initial awareness of Christianity
		−7	Interest in Christianity
	Proclamation	−6	Awareness of basic facts of the Gospel
		−5	Grasp of implications of the Gospel
		−4	Positive attitude to the Gospel
	Persuasion	−3	Awareness of personal need
		−2	Challenge and decision to act
Regeneration		−1	Repentance and faith

A New Disciple Is Born — **Matthew 28:19-20**

Sanctification		+1	Evaluation of decision
		+2	Initiation into the church
		+3	Become part of the process of making other disciples
		•	Growth in understanding of the faith
		•	Growth in Christian character
		•	Discovery and use of gifts
		•	Christian lifestyle
		•	Stewardship of resources
		•	Prayer
		•	Openness to others
		•	Effective sharing of faith and life

Adapted from *What's Gone Wrong with the Harvest?* by James F. Engel and Wilbert Norton (Grand Rapids, Mich.: Zondervan, 1975). Figure from *Power Evangelism* by John Wimber and Kevin Springer. Copyright © 1986 by John Wimber and Kevin Springer. Reprinted by permission of Harper Collins Publishers.

I surrendered my life to Jesus during a Christian concert was the culmination of over two years of God working in my life.

Investigative Bible studies enable us to understand where people are and gives them time to continue moving, however slowly, toward becoming a Christian.

5

Going Fishing

When my wife and I started New Life Fellowship in New York City, the church we presently pastor, we had one serious problem—no people! My ministry had been completely in Spanish for the preceding two years. As a result, we had very few contacts for an English-speaking church.

We prayed (very desperately) and began making a prospect list of potential people. Through one of my friends, I met a chaplain at Elmhurst Hospital, one of the largest hospitals in New York City. He shared with me how unresponsive people, especially staff, were to the gospel, and about his plans for retirement in the next few months.

With thousands of employees, I figured there must be some responsive people there, so I asked him if I could lead a Bible study for staff in the hospital. He didn't think anyone would come, but agreed to a three-week probationary period.

The first week seven people came. In the second week fifteen wandered into the room. By the third week, Denise, a very friendly head nurse, had become a Christian, and twenty-five people came to the study!

God used that lunchtime study in the next few months to give me countless contacts with interested unchurched people and to help launch New Life Fellowship.

For the next few months I led investigative Bible studies in any home, work place or park where God opened a door. My prayer each week was very simple: "Father, lead me to people you have prepared, by the Holy Spirit, to be responsive to the Word."

He did. And a new church was birthed!

Practical Steps for Getting Started

1. *Pray in faith.* Remember the disciples' unsuccessful attempt to heal the epileptic boy with a demon in Mark 9:14-32. When they asked Jesus why they were unable to drive it out, his response was: "This kind can come out only by prayer" (v. 29). In the Gospel account of Matthew, Jesus adds "Because you have so little faith. I tell you the truth, if you have faith as small as a mustard seed, you can say to this mountain, 'Move from here to there' and it will move. Nothing will be impossible for you" (Mt 17:20).

Ask the Lord with confidence, like the apostle Paul, to open a door for the message of Jesus (Col 4:3) and to give you great boldness (Eph 6:19). Pray this every day and watch God set up "divine appointments" for you. Jesus said the harvest is great, but the laborers few—and it really is.

Ask others in the body of Christ to stand with you in prayer. You are involving yourself in a battle with the powers of darkness who do not want to lose control of any territory (in this case—people). Be sure to enlist the prayer support of your church or campus fellowship. You may even want to fast and pray for one meal or one day a week.

Expect God to do a great work in your midst. Jesus encouraged us to pray boldly: "I tell you the truth, my Father will give you whatever you ask in my name. Until now you have not asked for anything in my name. Ask and you will receive, and your joy will be complete" (Jn 16:23-24).

2. *Ask God if there is another believer you can work with.* It is usually a great help to have a second Christian in the group, especially when the group is more than five people. Ecclesiastes 4:9-12 says, "Two are better than one, because they have a good return for their work: If one falls down, his friend can help him up. But pity the man who falls and has no one to help him up! . . . Though one may be overpowered, two can defend themselves. A cord of three strands is not quickly broken." The key is to find a brother or sister who is sensitive to the Holy Spirit and the needs of the people you are inviting.

3. *Make a list of all the non-Christians you know on a first-name basis.* Think through all your relationships in your family, at work or school, in your neighborhood or dormitory, among your friends and in any social or professional organizations. To expand your list, think of non-Christians you may have met at church-sponsored activities, special programs, or through a church worship service. Ask other people in your fellowship or church for referrals. The following are areas where you have potential contacts:

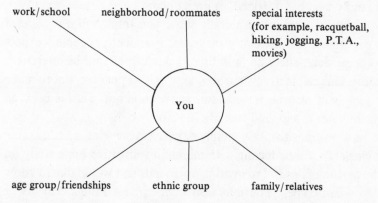

Pray over your list regularly, asking God for direction and wisdom. Go through the list slowly in prayer with a listening ear. We serve a God who desires to speak to us.

4. *Add to your list by attending or creating "fishing pond" events to make new friendships.* Our church regularly sponsors "fishing pond" events such as concerts, movies, dinners and picnics to draw out new people and to help believers develop relationships with non-Christians. Support groups, canoe trips, Vacation Bible School, aerobic classes and marriage retreats are only a few of the limitless possibilities for meeting new people and giving the Holy Spirit the opportunity for him to knit you with others.

5. *Build genuine friendships with the people you are inviting.* Above all, you want to communicate sincere caring and love. Many people are wounded due to problems like sickness, financial instability, family difficulties or stress. Caring involves listening, getting involved in their struggles and concerns, being available even when it is not convenient. Even inviting people to your home for dinner can go a long way.

In fact, a well-known church growth principle is that people are most responsive to a change in their lifestyle during periods of time when their everyday lives are disrupted by an irregular event such as a divorce, birth of a child, a job transfer or move, the death of a family member or friend, or even holidays.[2]

6. *Invite everyone,* especially those you think will not come. I have often been pleasantly surprised. Frequently, people I expect to come don't show up, and those I don't think will be interested, come. Our call is to sow the seed as widely as possible, not to make a judgment on who is good soil and who is not. That is between the individual and God (see Mk 4:1-20).

In a very positive way simply say: "Next week at _____ o'clock we will be having a 45-minute investigative Bible study on the person of Jesus. I'm inviting my friends and would like to know if you can come." You may also want to mail announcements or make up a poster.

7. *Prepare the study well.* You will be glad you did, for as Proverbs teaches: "The plans of the diligent lead to profit as surely as haste leads to poverty" (Prov 21:5).

Let God speak to you in a fresh way each time you interact with the text. Ask and expect God to reveal something new of the unsearchable riches of Christ in the passage (Eph 3:8). Remember the Bible is like an ocean—shallow enough for a baby to wade in it yet deep enough for an elephant to drown.

8. *Remind those you have invited.* A follow-up phone call a few days or hours before the study is often very helpful. If you're in a dormitory or neighborhood, you may want to pick up those who have expressed an interest in attending.

9. *Create an inviting atmosphere.* I suggest you have refreshments before or at the beginning of your study. This establishes a friendly atmosphere and enables the latecomer to enter into the study without feeling left out. With an atmosphere of warmth and acceptance, you can easily get feedback by asking after the first study, "What did you think of our time together? Do you have any suggestions of what we could improve the next time?"

6

Keeping the
Fish Biting

While getting your friends and family to the investigative Bible study is one thing, to keep them interested for three or four weeks, remember to *communicate love.* A famous proverb rightly states: "People don't care how much we know until they know how much we care." Going out of your way to create an atmosphere of love and acceptance is essential.

If Paul were writing 1 Corinthians 13:1 in light of an investigative Bible study, he might say: "If I lead the best Bible study, knowing all the answers to the many questions I am asked, and if I do everything right, but have not love, I am nothing." Ask God to fill you with the love of Jesus for each group member. Remember that "love covers over a multitude of sins" (1 Pet 4:8).

Guidelines for the Study
To make the study a positive experience for those who come, you also need to keep some important leadership skills in mind.

Establish clear guidelines before beginning each study. If you do not establish ground rules at the outset of your time together, you will probably not reach your goal of introducing people to the Jesus of the New Testament. Imagine a Jew, an agnostic, a know-it-all religion major, a domineering Muslim and an open neighbor in the same study. The ground rules ensure you will at least expose them to one aspect of the person of Jesus before you go off on other subjects.

The following are suggested guidelines to explain to the group before beginning each study:

1. The Bible is the source of authority, not the leader. As questions surface, look to the text for the answer.

2. Stay on the topic under discussion. After the study is officially over, we can go off into unrelated topics.

3. This is a discussion, not a lecture. Everyone is encouraged to participate. If you tend to talk a lot, please be sensitive to the quieter persons in the group. If you tend to be on the quieter side, we want to encourage you to participate. Our desire is to have a balanced discussion.

4. Let's keep to the time limit of 45 minutes (or an hour if you like). At that point we will end the study.

You may find that people want to stay and ask questions. Be sure to officially close your time together so that people who want only the 45-minute study feel free to leave. Many people make the mistake of extending the first study to three hours and are left wondering why over half the group didn't return for the next meeting.

You will want to decide beforehand how long you will meet together. I usually suggest that the group commit itself to meet three times for one hour. After that the group evaluates together whether they want to continue for another two or three weeks.

Deal Wisely with Difficult People

The goal of the study is to have a balanced discussion, with each member of the group participating equally. The problem, however, is that you're dealing with unique individuals, each with their own history, personality and reasons for being there. If you lead many investigative studies you will inevitably encounter the following people:

Danny Dominant. This person answers almost all your questions and acts as if the others in the group aren't in the room. Your other friends in the room will communicate their frustration by rolling their eyes, hoping you'll do something. At times you can simply take stronger leadership of the study by asking, "What do the rest of you think? Any other comments or ideas?" In other situations you will need to talk to the person outside of the study, explaining again the guidelines and purpose of the study.

Terry Tangent. She has the ability to take the greatest study and lead it off-track into a tangent. Asking questions like, "What about the pygmies in Africa?" "What do you think about the pope's view on birth control?" "You don't really think Jonah was swallowed by a whale, do you?" "How could a loving God allow such suffering in the world?"

You respond to these questions with something like: "That's a great question, but it doesn't have to do with our topic now. Would it be okay if we talked about it after the study?" You may also want to ask if anyone else was wondering about the same issues and take time later that evening to talk together.

Don't be afraid to say "I don't know" to difficult questions. It is a healthy expression of humility and communicates more truth about Christianity than pretending to know everything.

Sammy Silent. Silence can be a healthy element in a study when people are looking into the text. Be patient and not afraid of it. You may want to draw out members who don't talk by addressing them personally: "Sammy, what do you think?" or "Sammy, what do you observe about Jesus in verses 2-3?" Again, you need to be sensitive to each person, respecting where they are and what God is doing in each.

Wayne Wrong Answer. This person seems to give wrong, and

even unbiblical, answers to even the simplest questions. At times
you can restate the question or ask another question that will enable you to move on in the study. You can say, "All right. What do
others of you think?" But you don't want to embarrass Wayne or
get trapped in a tangent.

Be Sensitive to the Holy Spirit

Evangelism in the ministry of Jesus and the early church included
both a proclamation and demonstration of the gospel. "Jesus went
through all the towns and villages, teaching in their synagogues,
preaching the good news of the kingdom and healing every disease
and sickness" (Mt 9:35).

The term *power evangelism* has been coined for this. John
Wimber has defined it as a "spontaneous, Spirit-inspired empow-
ered presentation of the gospel. Power evangelism is preceded and
undergirded by supernatural demonstrations of God's presence."[1]

In the context of investigative Bible studies, it means being open
to take time at the end of a meeting to pray for people as God might
lead you. For example, if someone is physically or emotionally sick,
ask them if you could pray for them. (Most people are thrilled that
you would care enough to pray.) Or if someone's marriage is in on
the brink of divorce, I might say, "God is in the business of restor-
ing broken marriages. Could I pray for you, asking God to bring
healing to your relationship, breathing love into the two of you for
one another?" I have rarely been refused. (For further information
on this theme, read *Authority to Heal* by Ken Blue [IVP].)

---

[1] John Wimber with Kevin Springer, *Power Evangelism* (New York:
Harper and Row, 1986), p. 35.

7

Catching Fish

James Kennedy in his classic *Evangelism Explosion* notes that 95
per cent of church members have never led a person to Jesus
Christ.[1] But if you are faithful in sowing the seed of God's Word,
he *will* give you a harvest. Jesus himself said, "I tell you, open your
eyes and look at the fields! They are ripe for harvest" (Jn 4:35).

For the first three years of my Christian life, whenever I knew
someone on the verge of committing their lives to Jesus, I would
get nervous and tense. I didn't know what to do. However, in
leading investigative studies, I have learned how to help people
make the commitment.

After a few weeks of being together, I have found it helpful to
sometimes explain the gospel to the entire group toward the end of
a meeting. (If there is only one person open to becoming a Christian, I meet with him or her at another time.) I distribute a well-
written gospel tract such as Campus Crusade's *Four Spiritual
Laws,* Billy Graham's *Steps to Peace with God,* or Evangelism
Explosion's *Do You Know for Sure That You Are Going to Be
with God in Heaven?*

I might say, "Tonight, as part of our time together, I'd like to take a few minutes to share with you what it means to have a personal relationship with Jesus Christ—what it means to be a Christian as explained by the New Testament." As we read through the booklet together, I make comments, give further explanations, and invite questions.

At other times I write out and/or explain the four points of the gospel—God's purpose, our condition of sin, Jesus' solution, and our response. This personalizes the presentation of the gospel. The following are some brief summary statements with Scripture references that you can use in sharing the gospel:

1. *God's purpose.* God, who created all things, loves you and has a plan for your life.

☐ "So God created man in his own image, in the image of God he created him; male and female he created them" (Gen 1:27).

☐ "I have come that they may have life, and have it to the full" (Jn 10:10).

God is just and holy. He punishes evil and must banish it from his presence.

☐ "God is light; in him there is no darkness at all" (1 Jn 1:5).

☐ "The wrath of God is being revealed from heaven against all the godlessness and wickedness of men who suppress the truth by their wickedness" (Rom 1:18).

2. *Our need.* God made us to be in relationship with him that we might find our purpose and joy in him.

☐ "For by him all things were created: things in heaven and on earth, visible and invisible, whether thrones or powers or rulers or authorities; all things were created by him and for him" (Col 1:16).

All of us have rebelled and gone our own way.

☐ "All have sinned and fall short of the glory of God" (Rom 3:23).

☐ "We all, like sheep, have gone astray, each of us has turned to his own way" (Is 53:6).

The result is separation from God and spiritual death.

☐ "Your iniquities have made a separation between you and your God, and your sins have hid his face from you so that he does not hear" (Is 59:2).

☐ "For the wages of sin is death" (Rom 6:23).

3. *Christt, the solution.* God became human in the person of Jesus Christ to die for us and restore our broken relationship with him. Christ paid the penalty of our sin and rose from the dead.

☐ "But God demonstrates his own love for us in this: While we were still sinners, Christ died for us" (Rom 5:8).

☐ "I am the way and the truth and the life. No one comes to the Father except through me" (Jn 14:6).

☐ "He was raised on the third day according to the Scriptures" (1 Cor 15:4).

4. *Our response.* There are four key parts to our response:

☐ We must admit our need to God. (I am a sinner.)

☐ We must be willing to turn from our sins to him as Lord.

☐ We must believe Jesus Christ died for our sins and was resurrected.

☐ We must, through prayer, receive Jesus Christ to come in and control our lives.

☐ "Yet to all who received him, to those who believed in his name, he gave the right to become children of God" (Jn 1:12).

☐ "Here I am! I stand at the door and knock. [Christ is speaking.] If anyone hears my voice and opens the door, I will come in and eat with him, and he with me" (Rev 3:20).

At the end of the presentation, I lead those who are interested in a prayer to receive Jesus as their Lord and Savior.

It is extremely important that we learn to share not only Jesus' story, but also our own testimonies. Paul used his testimony in defending the gospel on at least two occasions (Acts 22; 26). Peter and John also knew the power of personal testimony: "We cannot help speaking about what we have seen and heard" (Acts 4:20).

While we are not asking people to believe because of our personal experiences alone, our stories do validate the truth of the gospel. It exclaims with authority, "Jesus is alive and has changed my life. He can change your life too." Who could argue with the blind man who said, "Whether he is a sinner or not, I don't know. One thing I do know. I was blind but now I can see" (Jn 9:25)?

Don't feel like you need to always give your personal testimony. Let the Holy Spirit lead you. However, take time to think through your spiritual autobiography so that you can honestly and briefly share it when God opens the door. The following is an outline I've found helpful:

1. What I was like before I became a Christian.

2. What God used to begin to open my eyes (circumstances, people and so on).

3. How I came to know Christ (that is, what aspect of the gospel touched me).

4. How Christ has changed my life since that time (relationships, attitudes, goals and desires).

Trust in the Spirit

We need both great boldness and great sensitivity to the Holy Spirit as we call people to repentance and faith in Jesus Christ. If you step out in faith at the middle or toward the end of your investigative Bible study series to challenge people to Christ, often you will find that the Holy Spirit has gone before you. May God teach us to cooperate with his Holy Spirit in the work of drawing a person to Christ, that the "Word of God might grow mightily and prevail" (Acts 19:20).

---

[1]James Kennedy, *Evangelism Explosion* (Wheaton, Ill.: Tyndale, 1983), p. 4.

8

Six Weeks
of Bible Studies

Now you've done all the groundwork, and you have a group of people assembled who want to learn about Christ. What will you study together?

The following studies will help you get started. They will provide a good introduction to who Jesus is, what the Bible is about, and what it takes to be a follower of Christ.

Using the Studies

This guide has been designed for the leader's convenience. Each study includes a purpose statement, an introduction, background information where needed. The study questions are followed by notes and commentary to help you through the study.

Before each study, prayerfully read the biblical material several times to prepare. Give God time to speak to you personally. Pray for the Holy Spirit to drive the truths of the passage into the people who will be attending.

Take your time in reading through the questions and notes. There is extra space after each question for you to add your own notes.

Feel free to omit, add or adapt the questions to help your particular group. These questions are meant to serve you. Make each study your own, asking God for wisdom (Jas 1:5).

The material you will read aloud to the group is in bold typeface. The background information and the purpose statement appear in italics and are for your use. So are the notes and instructions in a small typeface. Do not read these out loud in the group. Occasionally, you may want to rephrase some of this information to help the group along.

At the end of the book are copies of the studies without the notes that you can photocopy and distribute to your group.

Although the studies are arranged in a reasonable sequence, please feel free to use them in whatever order will best meet the group's needs.

As you lead, learn and enjoy. And may God, knowing we are very much jars of clay as we lead these studies, spread everywhere the fragrance of the knowledge of his Son (2 Cor 2:14; 4:7).

Study 1

Are You Ready?

John the Baptist

Luke 3:2-18

Note: Read out loud or paraphrase for the group what is in bold type. Information in regular or italic type is background information for your use and should not be read out loud to the group.

Purpose: *To examine the nature of true repentance.*

In *A Christmas Carol* by Charles Dickens, Scrooge, a miserable and greedy man, is forced to confront his final destiny. In a dream he is taken on a journey where he sees, with brutal clarity, his past, present and, most significantly, his dismal future. Scrooge awakens a frightened but changed man.

Many of us live such busy lives that we have little time for reflection on the whole of our lives. Occasionally a person or an event, such as a death, will cause us to pause and reconsider our lives from a fresh perspective. John the Baptist was one such person.

Background: Before the study, you may want to read Mark 1:1-8 and Luke 1:5-25, 57-66 for more information about John the Baptist. History tells us that the political and religious leaders mentioned in the first two verses were corrupt, ruthless and powerful. John, on the other hand, cared little for people's social or religious position. While their authority came from the force of the Roman Empire and religious education, the authority of John was due to the word of God having come to him (vv. 1-2).

---

1. At what times of the year or at what events do you re-examine your life and future? Explain.

The first question of each study is an *approach question*. This question is designed to orient the group to the theme of the study. It should be read before the Scripture passage is read. It will help them to begin to open up to each other in a non-threatening way. Allow time for as many people in the group as feel comfortable to respond.

---

2. John the Baptist was someone who helped people evaluate their lives. At the time of this passage the Jewish people are living under the control of the Roman Empire. In the midst of their oppression appears John. As we observe him speaking to the crowds in the first century, he speaks to us today.

Have members of the group read aloud Luke 3:2-18.

What do you learn about John and his message from verses 2-3?

If people have trouble answering, ask them to paint the scene at the river Jordan as vividly as possible. They may picture thousands of people, the humiliation of being completely submerged in water by this strange, oddly dressed fellow named John.

This can be a difficult question since verses 2-3 are filled with theological words. You may want to ask them, "What do *you* think it means to repent?" before giving some explanation. The word *repentance* means literally "a change of mind." It involves a completely new direction, a return to God and a 180-degree moral U-turn. You can illustrate this by standing up, walking in one direction, and making a U-turn. Don't spend too much time defining repentance here, however, since this is the theme of the study.

"A baptism of repentance" meant that a person would be immersed or dipped completely in the river Jordan by John. This would symbolize repentance before God, that is, willingness to turn away from sin and wrongdoing.

---

3. Luke quotes from an Old Testament prophecy written over 700 years before John's time to help us understand his ministry (vv. 4-6). What images do verses 4-6 use to show what needs to be done in order to prepare for the coming Messiah—Jesus?

The author quotes Isaiah 40:3-5, noting that the purpose of John's preparation is to shout in the wilderness that men and women must prepare the way for the Lord (see 1:76) and make straight paths for him. The image is the construction of a level road making it easy for the coming king (the Messiah, Jesus) to travel.

---

4. What might be a crooked road that needs to become straight or a mountain that needs to be made level in someone's life?

Some possibilities might be pride, love of money, sexual immorality or drug use. Be sure, however, to note that it is not that I clean up my life before coming to Jesus. Repentance, rather, is a willingness to turn from these things to Jesus.

---

5. John calls the large crowds coming out to him for baptism a group of poisonous snakes ("you brood of vipers"). Why does he

speak so harshly to them (vv. 7-9)?

6. The people are saying, "We're okay. We have Abraham as our father" (v. 8). How does he respond to their overconfidence regarding their religious heritage?

This is a key question. Many of the Jews felt they were fine before God because Abraham was their father. John says that without an inward change of heart evidenced by outward fruit, religion is meaningless.

7. What are some ways that people today say, "I'm okay with God"?

Many people today say, "I'm okay with God. I'm a good person" or "I'm a good _____" (insert the name of your denomination or church). Be careful about how you handle this sensitive question.

8. What do the questions the people ask in verses 10-14 reveal about them?

Even the poor had two tunics. One was an outer garment, the other an undergarment for the night cold.

Tax collectors were hated by fellow Jews and considered ritually unclean. They regularly overcollected taxes and were thus placed in the same class as prostitutes.

Roman soldiers were not well paid and, as a result, were subject to the tremendous temptation to extort money from the Jews by intimidation. This was probably a common practice. As a result the soldiers were privileged, powerful and hated.

How does John respond to each question (vv. 10-14)?

Note that he didn't tell them to change jobs.

_____

9. What do his answers teach us about genuine repentance (see also v. 8)?

_____

10. Describe the thoughts and feelings of the people in verse 15.

_____

11. Only a Gentile (non-Jewish) slave was expected to untie the thongs of a master's sandals, never a Jew. What do we learn about John and Jesus from his response in verses 16-17?

_____

12. How will the baptism of Jesus be different from the baptism of John?

"The chaff represents the unrepentant and the wheat the righteous. Many Jews thought that only pagans would be judged and punished when the Messiah came, but John declared that judgment would come to all who did not repent—including the Jews" (Kenneth Barker, *The NIV Study Bible* [Grand Rapids, Mich.: Zondervan, 1985], p. 1541).

_____

13. Why is repentance (that is, turning around) necessary to becoming a Christian?

14. At this point in your life, what is an obstacle that keeps you from being ready to follow Jesus?

You'll need to determine whether your group is ready for this question. You may want to ask the question rhetorically—giving it to them as something to think about, but not answer aloud.

Study 2

What Is on Your Heart?

The Parable of the Sower

Mark 4:1-20

*Note: Read out loud or paraphrase for the group what is in bold type.
Information in regular or italic type is background information for your
use and should not be read out loud to the group.*

**Purpose: To consider the kind of heart necessary to receive Jesus and to
help people in the group analyze where they are in their relationship with
Jesus.**

"I'm not the religious type."

**"My friends would think I was crazy if I became fanatical like
you."**

"How do I know Christianity will work for me?"

**"I think Jesus was the Son of God. The problem is that I don't
have time to follow him."**

**Since Jesus began his public ministry over 1900 years ago, his
message has been proclaimed on every continent in the world. With
each person, and for different reasons, the response to him has been
different.**

1. When in your life have you felt closest to God? Why?

___

2. In the parable of the sower Jesus talks about some of the reasons people respond to him in different ways.

Have members of the group read aloud Mark 4:1-20.

Describe what happens with each type of soil the farmer scatters seed on and why (vv. 4-8).

You only want group members to describe what happened physically at this point. The interpretation will come in verses 14-20.

___

3. Jesus calls out in verse 9, "He who has ears to hear, let him hear" and then apparently walks away without explaining the meaning of the parable. Why do you think the "the Twelve and the others" (v. 10) come to ask for the meaning of the parable while the rest of the crowd does not?

Jesus did not explain the parable to everyone, only to those who came and asked him the meaning. Help the group to see that these people were the "good soil." The rest of the crowd, however, heard Jesus, but didn't really understand (see v. 12).

You may want to ask the group: "If you were in the crowd and only heard verses 3-8, would you have gone after Jesus to find out the meaning of the parable?"

___

4. What does Jesus promise them as a result (vv. 11-12)?

"The secret of the kingdom" is that in the person of Jesus, the kingdom of God had come (William Lane, *Commentary on the Gospel of Mark* [Grand Rapids, Mich.: Eerdmans, 1974], p. 158). The disciples are able to see this. However, unbelief and disinterest causes people's eyes to be blinded and ears to be dulled; Jesus makes no sense to them.

---

5. Jesus begins explaining the parable in verse 13. What happens to the seed along the path?

What are some ways that the Bible is taken away from people today?

After others answer, you may want to mention specific people you have known that illustrate each type of soil in case the group members have difficulty. Be careful not to offend anyone, but paint as vivid a picture as possible.

---

6. What happens to the seed sown on rocky places?

Describe a modern person who receives the Word with joy, but lasts only a short time.

---

7. What happens to the seed that falls among thorns?

What are the "worries of this life" and desires (v. 19) that prevent you from following Christ?

8. What happens to the seed that is sown on good soil?

What would a person who is good soil today be like?

_____

9. Which of these four soils best describes the state of your heart? Explain.

Leave sufficient time for these application questions.

_____

10. What do you think Jesus might be saying to you through this parable?

Study 3

The Power of the Kingdom

A Day in the Life of Jesus

Mark 1:15-34

Note: Read out loud or paraphrase for the group what is in bold type. Information in regular or italic type is background information for your use and should not be read out loud to the group.

Purpose: *To reflect on the authority and power of Jesus and its implications for our lives.*

On D-Day, June 6, 1944, millions of Allied soldiers invaded Europe in order to recapture territory under the hold of Hitler. That successful invasion broke the power of Nazi Germany. From that point forward, everyone knew it was only a matter of time before Hitler would surrender and the war would end.

In the same way, the New Testament describes the coming of Jesus as an invasion of the kingdom of God—a spiritual assault against evil and demonic powers.

1. What comes to your mind when you think of a king and a kingdom? Explain.

2. In this description of a day in the life of Jesus, the writer Mark gives us a portrait of the power and nature of the kingdom of God. Jesus begins his ministry with the message: "The time has come. The kingdom of God is near. Repent and believe the good news" (Mk 1:15).

Have members of the group read aloud Mark 1:16-34.

In verses 16-20, Jesus calls four men. What does he call them to?

The call of Jesus on these four men was one of discipleship. It implied breaking all other ties to follow him.

What is their response?

James and John left their father, the hired servants, the boat and the nets behind in a step of radical obedience. Consider what a step of faith this was and what their friends and family might have said!

Moreover, it was characteristic in Jesus' day that a disciple would choose a rabbi or master. Here Jesus chooses them (see Jn 15:16). He promises that he will make them become something they are not right now—fishers of men.

Help the group consider the implications for their families, personal lives, businesses and future.

3. What three incidents are described in verses 21-34?

First, while Jesus is teaching in the synagogue, he is confronted by an evil spirit (v. 23). Second, Jesus heals Simon's mother-in-law (vv. 29-31). Third, Jesus heals other diseases and drives out demons outside Simon's house (vv. 32-33).

4. Imagine yourself sitting in the synagogue described in verses 21-27. What would you see, hear and feel?

5. How is Jesus' teaching different from that of the Jewish teachers of his day?

The teachers of the Law were the recognized interpreters of the Law, that is, the Old Testament, and were deeply revered and honored by the common people. They functioned as legal experts, applying the Law to people's everyday lives. Thus we see that Jesus, while he was not ordained from one of the recognized rabbinical schools, taught with an incredible prophetic authority from God.

6. What two things about Jesus amazed the people (v. 27)?

7. What impresses you most about Jesus in Simon's house (vv. 29-31)?

Jesus' mercy and concern reaches even to individuals in their homes—in this case, Simon's mother-in-law. In response to her healing, she immediately rises up to serve Jesus.

8. Compare the healing of Simon's mother in-law with the driving out of the demon in verses 21-28. What do they have in common?

9. Describe the scene that evening at Simon and Andrew's door from the perspective of a reporter from the "Capernaum News" (vv. 32-34).

10. Why do you think he silenced the demons (v. 34)?

Demons are powerless before the authority of the king—Jesus—and his power. With only a few words Jesus silences them. Jesus apparently had a timetable for his mission which caused him to silence not only demons, but also those healed (1:44-45) and even the disciples (8:30). Perhaps the crowds would have so overwhelmed him that it would have been impossible for him to complete the call of the Father for him. Another explanation might be that he did not want demons giving testimony to his person.

11. What do these three incidents reveal to us about the authority of Jesus and the kingdom of God?

It is important to note that the kingdom of God is not just a message of forgiveness, but it is also a work. Ken Blue in *Authority to Heal* notes: "When Christ began his public ministry, he immediately engaged the enemy in battle and won victories over him. Jesus' conquest over Satan was evidenced in the casting out of demons, healing the sick and raising the dead. Satan continually lost ground against the advance of Christ's kingdom rule because Jesus had bound the strong man and was now plundering his house (Mt 12:29)" (p. 81).

12. Why is this such good news (v. 15) in a day like ours when so many people are hurting?

The reason the gospel is such good news is that Jesus has power to change people's lives—regardless of how desperate their situations might be. You may want to leave time at the end of the study to pray for people's needs.

---

13. Jesus is presented here as a king with authority over every area of life. What is your response to this authority?

You will need to be sensitive to the Holy Spirit and to the people in your group to determine how—or if—you should ask question 13.

Study 4

Looking for Something

The Samaritan Woman

John 4:4-26

Note: Read out loud or paraphrase for the group what is in bold type. Information in regular or italic type is background information for your use and should not be read out loud to the group.

Purpose: To encounter the person of Jesus as a source of satisfaction and rest.

From commercials to self-help seminars to TV, our environment shouts at us: "Pursue the Good Life." "Make yourself happy!" "You deserve only the best." The result is we often find ourselves preoccupied with celebrities, food, fancy automobiles, entertainment, hairstyles, weight loss, and clothes.

    Yet St. Augustine wrote, "Thou has made us for thyself, and we shall never find rest till we rest in Thee." In this study we meet Jesus as the One who goes out to show mercy to outcasts—tax collectors, prostitutes, sinners—as well as one who alone can fill that "God-shaped hole" in people's lives.

1. When you were growing up, what part of the country or city did your parents warn you against visiting? Explain.

---

2. In this passage Jesus explores our deepest needs as he travels through the "inner city" of his day.

Have members of the group read aloud John 4:4-26.

Jesus and his disciples were returning from Judea to Galilee and stopped to rest by a well. Jews were taught to hate the Samaritans because they were "half-Jews," having intermarried with the wrong families (Gentiles). How do you think the disciples felt when Jesus decided to go through Samaria instead of around it?

The sixth hour is about noon.

The hate between Jews and Samaritans went back centuries, going back to the origins of the Samaritans as a mixed race who intermarried with Gentiles (see 2 Kings 17:24-41). The bitterness between Jews and Samaritans was at its height in the time of Jesus. Jews considered their presence in the temple to be cursed and their food unclean. Nonetheless, the Samaritans viewed themselves as the true Israel and heirs of God's promises!

---

3. Jesus overcame several powerful prejudices of his day to talk to this woman—*social* (Jewish men didn't speak to women in public, v. 9), *moral* (Jews particularly avoided immoral women, v. 20) and *religious* (Samaritans and Jews did not associate, v. 27). What might have motivated Jesus to have a conversation with an immoral woman from a despised race?

Jewish women in Jesus' day did not take part in public life. They were expected to wear veils in public and spend most of their lives at home. They were excluded from formal education (it was only for boys). Moreover, women were only allowed in the court of the Gentiles in the temple area and were not even considered worthy to bless food at table meals.

This is what makes Jesus asking a Samaritan for a drink, having a conversation with this immoral woman, and evangelizing the area so incredible. In terms of race, religion and gender, she is a hated outsider.

_____

4. What kinds of people do we tend to avoid and why?

_____

5. What is the woman's first reaction to Jesus when he draws her into conversation (vv. 7-9)?

_____

6. What do you think Jesus meant by the "living water" he describes in verses 10-15?

In the Mideastern culture of Jesus' day, water was an absolute necessity for life. "Living water" was a common expression for flowing or spring water. Jesus is both the source of living water and the one who gives the water of life to those who are thirsty (see Jn 7:37-39). The living water of Jesus continually satisfies our need for a relationship with God. While we may seek other substitutes, it is Jesus alone who can satisfy.

_____

7. What does he say will be the result of drinking the water he gives (vv. 13-14)?

8. How does Jesus turn the conversation to her personal life (vv. 15-18)?

_____

9. What is the relationship between her past history and the thirst Jesus is speaking about?

_____

10. What are some ways people (include yourself here!) today seek to fill the emptiness of their lives?

In order to fill the emptiness in her life this woman apparently went from relationship to relationship. Think through the things your group may be relying on to fill the emptiness within them (for example, career, sex, sports, success and recognition, school and so on).

_____

11. How does Jesus treat the woman's attempt to enter into a religious argument about the "proper" place of worship (vv. 20-24)?

Jesus tells her the crucial question is not where but how to worship God. "True worshipers" will worship God as their Father "in spirit and truth," that is, from their hearts in the power of God's Spirit.

_____

12. What do you think were the things about Jesus in this encounter that caused the woman to become convinced Jesus was the Messiah?

You may want to also look at verses 28-29 and 39.

13. What impresses you about the person of Jesus in this passage?

Note that Jesus does not, after exposing her adultery, focus on her guilt. Rather, he speaks to the deep need within her for "living water" (that is, for something in life that satisfies). In the same way, focus on the false substitutes individuals in the group may be trusting in to fill the emptiness of their lives. Then point them to the tender love of Jesus for them in their present situation.

14. If Jesus were talking with you today, what might he say?

Study 5

Running Away from God

The Parable of the Prodigal Son

Luke 15:11-32

Note: Read out loud or paraphrase for the group what is in bold type. Information in regular or italic type is background information for your use and should not be read out loud to the group.

Purpose: To consider the love of the Father and to help the group enter into an experience of that love.

For some people God is like a *cop*. He is always watching us and waiting to see if we do something wrong. For others, he is like a *critical parent*. He can't be pleased. Trying to measure up to his impossible standard only leads to frustration. Still others imagine God as a *disinterested philosopher* who is too busy running the universe to be concerned with our small problems. In fact we think he has a sign outside his door saying, "Do Not Disturb."

1. Which of the following images best describes God to you: a policeman, a critical parent, an old gentleman, a faraway God in

the sky, or a loving father? Explain.

2. In this famous parable of the prodigal son, Jesus challenges the religious leaders of his day to set aside their prejudices and consider afresh what God is really like.

Have members of the group read aloud Luke 15:11-32.

According to Jewish law, a younger son would receive one-third of the entire inheritance. But to give it to him early was highly unusual. What do you think the father's neighbors and friends might have thought or said about this?

Since people normally married between 18 and 20 years old, the younger son was probably about 17 years old.

The Old Testament law decreed that the first-born son received two-thirds of the inheritance (Deut 21:17). The son gives no reason for his request. He takes his inheritance (which was probably a very large sum indeed) and immediately converts it to cash. This suggests he had no intention of returning.

3. The son finally gets a job feeding pigs to support himself. For a Jewish man this was "hitting the bottom." Their law said, "Cursed is the man who rears swine."[1] What do you think went through the young man's mind during this time (vv. 15-16)?

Feeding pigs was an occupation only for Gentiles. This was an unclean occupation for Jews and was as low as a Jew could go. [See I. Howard Marshall, *The Gospel of Luke,* New International Greek Testament Commentary (Grand Rapids, Mich.: Eerdmans, 1978), p. 608.] The desire to share their food represents that lowest point. Be sensitive to people in the group who might be able to relate to this experience of "hitting bottom."

4. What does the son realize when he "comes to his senses" (vv. 17-20)?

5. What are some of the reasons people who have run away from God finally turn back to him?

6. How might you have expected the father to respond to the son when he returned home?

7. Describe the reception the father gives the son in verses 20-24.

8. The best robe was reserved for the best guests. The ring was a symbol of authority which gave the son the right to buy and sell in his father's name. The shoes were a sign of wealth and freedom. What does each suggest about the love of God the Father?

The father brings out the best robe for the son to wear, robes appropriate to a son. In the same way God gives us the robes of righteousness in Christ (forgiveness). The ring was a symbol of royal authority enabling the son to act on behalf of his father. So are we able to act, pray and witness in the name of our Father. The shoes also were a sign he was a freeman, not a slave. They too indicated authority, freedom and the ability to walk in what the Father has for us.

9. What do the kisses, the embraces, the music and dancing for the son reveal about the feelings of our Father in heaven?

Make sure the group sees the incredible joy and love of the father for the son. He takes the initiative and runs to his son. He embraces and kisses him. This is not an unemotional God! He is filled with affection for his son who has returned home. Help them picture themselves at the table prepared by the father, with music and dancing all around them.

10. What is the older brother's reaction to this extravagant expression of joy over his brother's return (vv. 25-30)?

11. While he lives in the same house with the father, how is he too cut off and isolated from the love of the father?

12. How does the father treat the older son (vv. 28, 31-32)?

13. What is Jesus teaching here about repentance (turning to God) and the love of God?

The elder son represents the Pharisees and religious leaders of Luke 15:1-2 who were grumbling about Jesus spending so much time with tax collectors and sinners. Like many good religious people today who feel that they "have been slaving for God all these years and never disobeyed his orders" (v. 29), they missed the intimate love of the Father for them. They had a religion but not a relationship. If you have people in your group from "religious" backgrounds, you'll want to spend extra time dealing with the elder son.

---

14. Which of the two sons can you relate to most easily? Why?

---

15. Jesus leaves the reader wondering if the elder brother will go to the feast and eat. How can this portrait of God help you to enter in and receive his love despite your sin?

Many non-Christians believe "If I follow Jesus, he'll ruin my life." You may want to address that lie from the father of lies (Jn 8:44) with what Jesus says here in this parable.

---

[1]Leon Morris, *The Gospel According to St. Luke,* rev. ed. (Grand Rapids, Mich.: Eerdmans, 1988), p. 241.

Study 6

What Must I Do?

The Rich Young Ruler

Mark 10:17-31

Purpose: To understand the riches and the cost of entering the kingdom of God, challenging each member of the group to follow Jesus.

In the famous story entitled "Acres of Diamonds," a wealthy Persian with a large farm and gardens is told that diamonds are the last and highest of all mineral creations. As a result, he sells his farm, leaves his family and travels to the Mideast, Africa and Europe in search of this treasure. After many years, he eventually dies in poverty and misery. Years later, however, acres of the most magnificent diamonds of all history are discovered in the very estate the man had left behind. Had he realized what was within his reach, instead of poverty and death in a strange land, he would have enjoyed great wealth and success in his "acres of diamonds."

1. The chart below gives different stages in the spiritual journey of a person. Where are you now in your relationship with God? Explain.

Redraw the chart below or photocopy it so that the whole group can see it.

-7	-6	-5	-4	-3	-2	-1		+1	+2	+3
No interest	Who cares?	I'm open	Searching	Positive about Jesus	Recognize my need	Ready to decide	**Repentance and Faith**		Growth in Christ	

2. Jesus, in this conversation with a rich young ruler, speaks to many of us who are close to the riches of the kingdom of God.

Have members of the group read aloud Mark 10:17-31.

How does the man approach Jesus (v. 17)?

The rich man was eager (he runs up to Jesus), humble (kneeling), and respectful (calling a person "good" in those days was rare). Moreover, he sincerely wanted eternal life and was religious.

3. What does the verb "to do" (v. 17) suggest about his understanding of how to gain eternal life?

His focus was on what he should *do*. He was thinking of entering the kingdom of God based on his performance, not of receiving the kingdom as a gift from God in the helplessness of a child (see Mk 10:15).

4. How does Jesus respond to his question (vv. 18-19)?

"In calling in question the man's use of 'good,' Jesus' intention is not to pose the question of his own sinlessness or oneness with the Father, but to set in correct perspective the honor of God" (William L. Lane, *Com-*

mentary of the Gospel of Mark [Grand Rapids, Mich.: Eerdmans, 1974], pp. 365-66). The man mistakenly assumed, like many, that he had perfectly kept God's commandments.

---

5. Jesus gives the man a "pop quiz" on a partial list of the Ten Commandments, all of which relate to person-to-person relationships. What does the rich man's reply tell us about his view of himself (v. 20)?

Jesus mentions a partial listing of the Ten Commandments (see Ex 20:1-17), but applies only the first one to him: "You shall have no other gods before me" (Ex 20:3). For him, money had become a god.

---

6. What are the two parts of the command Jesus *lovingly* gives the rich man in verse 21?

Note that Jesus demand of this man is not a general rule to be applied to all potential followers. It was appropriate in this situation for two reasons. First, money had become this man's treasure, and in the kingdom of God no one can serve two masters (see Mt 6:24). Second, Jesus was seeking to reduce the man to helplessness in order that he might be able to receive the gift of eternal life. The focus of the two-part command, however, is on the summons to follow Jesus.

---

7. What does the man's reaction reveal about him (v. 22)?

---

8. Imagine that Jesus says to you: "One thing you lack is . . ." How

might he finish the sentence?

9. A Jewish person of that day regarded riches as an indicator of God's blessing and favor. Why does that make Jesus' remarks in verses 23-25 so startling?

10. Why do riches make it so difficult for a person to enter the kingdom of God?

Jesus understood that wealth creates a false sense of security and causes people to trust in it rather than in God. His reference to the camel and the eye of the needle is to be taken literally. A camel, the largest animal in Palestine, could not possibly enter through such a small opening. It was impossible! This realization alarmed the disciples in verse 26: "Who then can be saved?"

Jesus' reply is that salvation is a gift only God can give. It is nothing we can do. This was his point to the rich ruler as well.

11. On what basis is it possible for anyone—rich ruler or poor beggar—to enter the kingdom (see vv. 26-27)? Explain.

12. What wealth does Jesus promise to those who follow him (vv. 29-30)?

Why do you think he slips in the phrase "and with them persecutions" along with such wonderful promises?

_____

13. How would the statement that "the first shall be last and last first" apply to the disciples and to the rich young ruler?

_____

14. In what ways do you relate to the young ruler? Explain.

Resource
Studies to Hand Out

Study 1

Are You Ready?

John the Baptist

Luke 3:2-18

In *A Christmas Carol* by Charles Dickens, Scrooge, a miserable and greedy man, is forced to confront his final destiny. In a dream he is taken on a journey where he sees, with brutal clarity, his past, present and, most significantly, his dismal future. Scrooge awakens a frightened but changed man.

Many of us live such busy lives that we have little time for reflection on the whole of our lives. Occasionally a person or an event, such as a death, will cause us to pause and reconsider our lives from a fresh perspective. John the Baptist was one such person.

---

1. At what times of the year or at what events do you re-examine your life and future? Explain.

2. John the Baptist was someone who helped people evaluate their lives. At the time of this passage the Jewish people are living under the control of the Roman Empire. In the midst of their oppression appears John. As we observe him speaking to the crowds in the first century, he speaks to us today.

Read aloud Luke 3:2-18.

What do you learn about John and his message from verses 2-3?

3. Luke quotes from an Old Testament prophecy written over 700 years before John's time to help us understand his ministry (vv. 4-6). What images do verses 4-6 use to show what needs to be done in order to prepare for the coming Messiah—Jesus?

4. What might be a crooked road that needs to become straight or a mountain that needs to be made level in someone's life?

5. John calls the large crowds coming out to him for baptism a group of poisonous snakes ("you brood of vipers"). Why does he speak so harshly to them (vv. 7-9)?

6. The people are saying, "We're okay. We have Abraham as our father" (v. 8). How does he respond to their overconfidence regarding their religious heritage?

7. What are some ways that people today say, "I'm okay with God"?

8. What do the questions the people ask in verses 10-14 reveal about them? How does John respond to each question (vv. 10-14)?

9. What do his answers teach us about genuine repentance (see also v. 8)?

10. Describe the thoughts and feelings of the people in verse 15.

11. Only a Gentile (non-Jewish) slave was expected to untie the thongs of a master's sandals, never a Jew. What do we learn about John and Jesus from his response in verses 16-17?

12. How will the baptism of Jesus be different from the baptism of John?

13. Why is repentance (that is, turning around) necessary to becoming a Christian?

14. At this point in your life, what is an obstacle that keeps you from being ready to follow Jesus?

Taken from *Introducing Jesus: Starting an Investigative Bible Study for Seekers* ©1991 by Peter Scazzero and used by permission of InterVarsity Press, P.O. Box 1400, Downers Grove, IL 60515.

Study 2

What Is on Your Heart?

The Parable of the Sower

Mark 4:1-20

"I'm not the religious type."

"My friends would think I was crazy if I became fanatical like you."

"How do I know Christianity will work for me?"

"I think Jesus was the Son of God. The problem is that I don't have time to follow him."

Since Jesus began his public ministry over 1900 years ago, his message has been proclaimed on every continent in the world. With each person, and for different reasons, the response to him has been different.

1. When in your life have you felt closest to God? Why?

2. In the parable of the sower Jesus talks about some of the reasons people respond to him in different ways.

Read aloud Mark 4:1-20.

Describe what happens with each type of soil the farmer scatters seed on and why (vv. 4-8).

3. Jesus calls out in verse 9, "He who has ears to hear, let him hear" and then apparently walks away without explaining the meaning of the parable. Why do you think "the Twelve and the others" (v. 10) come to ask for the meaning of the parable while the rest of the crowd does not?

4. What does Jesus promise them as a result (vv. 11-12)?

5. Jesus begins explaining the parable in verse 13. What happens to the seed along the path?

What are some ways that the devil takes the word away from people today?

6. What happens to the seed sown on rocky places? Describe a modern person who receives the Word with joy, but lasts only a short time.

7. What happens to the seed that falls among thorns?

What are the "worries of this life" and desires (v. 19) that prevent you from following Christ?

8. What happens to the seed that is sown on good soil?

What would a person who is good soil today be like?

9. Which of these four soils best describes the state of your heart? Explain.

10. What do you think Jesus might be saying to you through this parable?

Taken from *Introducing Jesus: Starting an Investigative Bible Study for Seekers* ©1991 by Peter Scazzero and used by permission of InterVarsity Press, P.O. Box 1400, Downers Grove, IL 60515.

Study 3

The Power of the Kingdom

A Day in the Life of Jesus

Mark 1:15-34

On D-Day, June 6, 1944, millions of Allied soldiers invaded Europe in order to recapture territory under the hold of Hitler. That successful invasion broke the power of Nazi Germany. From that point forward, everyone knew it was only a matter of time before Hitler would surrender and the war would end.

In the same way, the New Testament describes the coming of Jesus as an invasion of the kingdom of God—a spiritual assault against evil and demonic powers.

---

1. What comes to your mind when you think of a king and a kingdom? Explain.

2. In this description of a day in the life of Jesus, the writer Mark gives us a portrait of the power and nature of the kingdom of God. Jesus begins his ministry with the message: "The time has come. The kingdom of God is near. Repent and believe the good news" (Mk 1:15).

Read aloud Mark 1:16-34.

In verses 16-20, Jesus calls four men. What does he call them to?

What is their response?

3. What three incidents are described in verses 21-34?

4. Imagine yourself sitting in the synagogue described in verses 21-27.

What would you see, hear and feel?

5. How is Jesus' teaching different from that of the Jewish teachers of his day?

6. What two things about Jesus amazed the people (v. 27)?

7. What impresses you most about Jesus in Simon's house (vv. 29-31)?

8. Compare the healing of Simon's mother in-law with the driving out of the demon in verses 21-28. What do they have in common?

9. Describe the scene that evening at Simon and Andrew's door from the perspective of a reporter from the "Capernaum News" (vv. 32-34).

10. Why do you think he silenced the demons (v. 34)?

11. What do these three incidents reveal to us about the authority of Jesus and the kingdom of God?

12. Why is this such good news (v. 15) in a day like ours when so many people are hurting?

13. Jesus is presented here as a king with authority over every area of life. What is your response to this authority?

Study 4

Looking for Something

The Samaritan Woman

John 4:4-26

From commercials to self-help seminars to TV, our environment shouts at us: "Pursue the Good Life." "Make yourself happy!" "You deserve only the best." The result is we often find ourselves preoccupied with celebrities, food, fancy automobiles, entertainment, hairstyles, weight loss, and clothes.

Yet St. Augustine wrote, "Thou has made us for thyself, and we shall never find rest till we rest in Thee." In this study we meet Jesus as the One who goes out to show mercy to outcasts—tax collectors, prostitutes, sinners—as well as One who alone can fill that "God-shaped hole" in people's lives.

1. When you were growing up, what part of the country or city did your parents warn you against visiting? Explain.

2. In this passage Jesus explores our deepest needs as he travels through the "inner city" of his day.

Read aloud John 4:4-26.

Jesus and his disciples were returning from Judea to Galilee and stopped to rest by a well. Jews were taught to hate the Samaritans because they were "half-Jews," having intermarried with the wrong families (Gentiles). How do you think the disciples felt when Jesus decided to go through

Samaria instead of around it?

3. Jesus overcame several powerful prejudices of his day to talk to this woman—*social* (Jewish men didn't speak to women in public, v. 9), *moral* (Jews particularly avoided immoral women, v. 20) and *religious* (Samaritans and Jews did not associate, v. 27). What might have motivated Jesus to have a conversation with an immoral woman from a despised race?

4. What kinds of people do we tend to avoid and why?

5. What is the woman's first reaction to Jesus when he draws her into conversation (vv. 7-9)?

6. What do you think Jesus meant by the "living water" he describes in verses 10-15?

7. What does he say will be the result of drinking the water he gives (vv. 13-14)?

8. How does Jesus turn the conversation to her personal life (vv. 15-18)?

9. What is the relationship between her past history and the thirst Jesus is speaking about?

10. What are some ways people (include yourself here!) today seek to fill the emptiness of their lives?

11. How does Jesus treat the woman's attempt to enter into a religious argument about the "proper" place of worship (vv. 20-24)?

12. What do you think were the things about Jesus in this encounter that caused the woman to become convinced Jesus was the Messiah?

13. What impresses you about the person of Jesus in this passage?

14. If Jesus were talking with you today, what might he say?

Study 5

Running Away from God

The Parable of the Prodigal Son

Luke 15:11-32

For some people God is like a *cop*. He is always watching us and waiting to see if we do something wrong. For others, he is like a *critical parent*. He can't be pleased. Trying to measure up to his impossible standard only leads to frustration. Still others imagine God as a *disinterested philosopher* who is too busy running the universe to be concerned with our small problems. In fact we think he has a sign outside his door saying, "Do Not Disturb."

1. Which of the following images best describes God to you: a policeman, a critical parent, an old gentleman, a faraway God in the sky, or a loving father? Explain.

2. In this famous parable of the prodigal son, Jesus challenges the religious leaders of his day to set aside their prejudices and consider afresh what God is really like.

Read aloud Luke 15:11-32.

According to Jewish law, a younger son would receive one-third of the entire inheritance. But to give it to him early was highly unusual. What do you think the father's neighbors and friends might have thought or said about this?

3. The son finally gets a job feeding pigs to support himself. For a Jewish man this was "hitting the bottom." Their law said, "Cursed is the man who rears swine."[1] What do you think went through the young man's mind during this time (vv. 15-16)?

4. What does the son realize when he "comes to his senses" (vv. 17-20)?

5. What are some of the reasons people who have run away from God finally turn back to him?

6. How might you have expected the father to respond to the son when he returned home?

7. Describe the reception the father gives the son in verses 20-24.

8. The best robe was reserved for the best guests. The ring was a symbol of authority which gave the son the right to buy and sell in his father's name. The shoes were a sign of wealth and freedom. What does each suggest about the love of God the Father?

9. What do the kisses, the embraces, the music and dancing for the son reveal about the feelings of our Father in heaven?

10. What is the older brother's reaction to this extravagant expression of joy over his brother's return (vv. 25-30)?

11. While he lives in the same house with the father, how is he too cut off and isolated from the love of the father?

12. How does the father treat the older son (vv. 28, 31-32)?

13. What is Jesus teaching here about repentance (turning to God) and the love of God?

14. Which of the two sons can you relate to most easily? Why?

15. Jesus leaves the reader wondering if the elder brother will go to the feast and eat. How can this portrait of God help you to enter in and receive his love despite your sin?

Taken from *Introducing Jesus: Starting an Investigative Bible Study for Seekers* ©1991 by Peter Scazzero and used by permission of InterVarsity Press, P.O. Box 1400, Downers Grove, IL 60515.

Study 6

What Must I Do?

The Rich Young Ruler

Mark 10:17-31

In the famous story entitled "Acres of Diamonds," a wealthy Persian with a large farm and gardens is told that diamonds are the last and highest of all mineral creations. As a result, he sells his farm, leaves his family and travels to the Mideast, Africa and Europe in search of this treasure. After many years, he eventually dies in poverty and misery. Years later, however, acres of the most magnificent diamonds of all history are discovered in the very estate the man had left behind. Had he realized what was within his reach, instead of poverty and death in a strange land, he would have enjoyed great wealth and success in his "acres of diamonds."

1. The chart below gives different stages in the spiritual journey of a person. Where are you now in your relationship with God? Explain.

-7	-6	-5	-4	-3	-2	-1		+1	+2	+3
No interest	Who cares?	I'm open	Searching	Positive about Jesus	Recognize my need	Ready to decide	**Repentance and Faith**		Growth in Christ	

2. Jesus, in this conversation with a rich young ruler, speaks to many of us who are close to the riches of the kingdom of God.

Read aloud Mark 10:17-31.

How does the man approach Jesus (v. 17)?

3. What does the verb "to do" (v. 17) suggest about his understanding of how to gain eternal life?

4. How does Jesus respond to his question (vv. 18-19)?

5. Jesus gives the man a "pop quiz" on a partial list of the Ten Commandments, all of which relate to person-to-person relationships. What does the rich man's reply tell us about his view of himself (v. 20)?

6. What are the two parts of the command Jesus *lovingly* gives the rich man in verse 21?

7. What does the man's reaction reveal about him (v. 22)?

8. Imagine that Jesus says to you, "One thing you lack is . . . ." How might he finish the sentence?

9. A Jewish person of that day regarded riches as an indicator of God's blessing and favor. Why does that make Jesus' remarks in verses 23-25 so startling?

10. Why do riches make it so difficult for a person to enter the kingdom of God?

11. On what basis is it possible for anyone—rich ruler or poor beggar—to enter the kingdom (see vv. 26-27)? Explain.

12. What wealth does Jesus promise to those who follow him (vv. 29-30)?

Why do you think he slips in the phrase "and with them persecutions" along with such wonderful promises?

13. How would the statement that "the first shall be last and last first" apply to the disciples and to the rich young ruler?

14. In what ways do you relate to the young ruler? Explain.

Further Reading

The following materials are particularly helpful when leading an investigative Bible study:

Arn, Win, and Charles Arn. *The Master's Plan for Making Disciples.* Pasadena, Calif.: Church Growth Press, 1982.

Aldrich, Charles. *Life Style Evangelism.* Portland, Ore.: Multnomah Press, 1981.

Dyrness, William. *Christian Apologetics in a World Community.* Downers Grove, Ill.: InterVarsity Press, 1983.

Eisenman, Tom L. *Everyday Evangelism.* Downers Grove, Ill.: InterVarsity Press, 1987.

Ford, Leighton. *Good News Is for Sharing.* Elgin, Ill.: David C. Cook, 1977.

Green, Michael. *Evangelism Now & Then.* Downers Grove, Ill.: InterVarsity Press.

Knectle, Cliff. *Give Me an Answer.* Downers Grove, Ill.: InterVarsity Press, 1986.

Lewis, C. S. *Mere Christianity.* New York: Macmillan, 1964.

Little, Paul. *How to Give Away Your Faith, Revised.* Downers Grove, Ill.: InterVarsity Press, 1988.

Peace, Richard. *Small Group Evangelism.* Downers Grove, Ill.: InterVarsity Press, 1985.

Wardle, Terry. *One to One: A Practical Guide to Friendship Evangelism.* Camp Hill, Penn.: 1989.

Watson, David. *I Believe in Evangelism.* Grand Rapids, Mich.: Eerdmans, 1976.

Wimber, John. *Power Evangelism.* San Francisco, Calif.: Harper and Row, 1986.

Bible Study Guides from InterVarsity Press

Any of the following LifeGuide® Bible Study Guides would provide a good follow-up to the studies in this book:

Connelly, Douglas. *John: The Way to True Life.* 26 studies in 2 parts. 1006-4.

Ford, Leighton. *Meeting Jesus.* 13 studies. 1060-9.

Offner, Hazel. *Fruit of the Spirit.* 9 studies. 1058-7.

Packer, J. I. *Meeting God.* 12 studies. 1057-9.

Sterk, Andrea, and Peter Scazzero. *Christian Character: Becoming the Person God Wants You to Be.* 12 studies. 1054-4.

Sterk, Andrea, and Peter Scazzero. *Christian Disciplines: Living the Way God Wants You to Live.* 12 studies. 1055-2.

Stott, John. *Sermon on the Mount.* 13 studies. 1036-6.

White, John. *Parables: The Greatest Stories Ever Told.* 12 studies. 1037-4.

Booklets from InterVarsity Press

These booklets will be helpful to you in leading people to Christ. They are also appropriate to give to non-Christians or new Christians.

Becker, Verne. *Safe Sex*. Factual summary of the physical and emotional consequences of sex outside marriage which shows that sex is always safest inside marriage and introduces the reader to God. 081-4.

Cassidy, Michael. *Christianity for the Open-Minded*. Cassidy confronts many of the problems doubters have as they look at the Christian faith. 170-5.

Colson, Charles W. *Why I Believe in Christ*. Colson describes how he came to faith, discusses his personal beliefs, and tells about the people who have influenced his faith significantly. 082-2.

Griffiths, Michael. *Encouraging New Christians*. Practical advice on how to help new Christians who want to develop mature faith. 106-3.

Groothuis, Douglas. *The New Age Movement*. Groothuis exposes the main beliefs of this movement, how it is organized and how Christians can respond. 079-2.

InterVarsity Staff. *Christ in You*. These introductory Bible studies discuss the basics of being a Christian and living a Christian life. 175-6.

Munger, Robert Boyd. *My Heart Christ's Home (rev)*. Christ's place in a person's life is compared to the rooms of a home to encourage Christians to be wholeheartedly devoted to Christ. 075-X.

Pippert, Rebecca Manley. *Pizza Parlor Evangelism*. A practical and humorous look at everyday evangelism. 169-1.

Smith, Wilbur. *Have You Considered Him?* Encourages honest inquiry into the historical claims of Jesus. 108-X

Stott, John R. W. *Becoming a Christian*. Stott discusses the fundamental human problem and the Christian answer to it, outlining the meaning of Christianity and specific steps a person can take to respond. 100-4.

_____ . *Being a Christian*. Stott describes the privileges of being a child of God and how one can develop to maturity in Christ. 101-2.